Royal
Invitation

How to Best Prepare yourself for Life's
Opportunities

Royal Invitation

How to Best Prepare yourself for Life's Opportunities

By Tunde Ogedengbe

Great Nation
Publishing House

Royal Invitation

How to Best Prepare yourself for Life's Opportunities

Great Nation Publishing House
Suite 9,
6 Union Street,
Luton, LU1 3AN
England

Tel: +44 (0) 1582 40 57 57
Fax: +44 (0) 1582 40 57 56

ISBN: 978-1-908259-00-4

Edited by: www.madeforministry.co.uk
Typeset and layout by: www.madeforministry.co.uk
Cover design by: www.madeforministry.co.uk

CONTENTS

DEDICATION

This book is dedicated to all of you out there who have waited for God to perform what He had promised you. Sometimes, I know, you think He has forgotten you. Alas! How can the God of the whole earth hold back on His promises? What we call 'delay' on earth is called 'process' there. You are in the preparation stage. Hold your breath! The delay is not a denial. It is a re-alignment, re-adjustment and re-positioning to qualify you for what He had promised you.

This book is also a part-payment to the debt I owe to all of you who have made a deposit in my life as instruments of God's working through the years. The work is not finished yet! Thank you for your input.

The first 'thank you' goes to 'Mummy', Mrs Adetoun Oladeji, also known as 'Mama ke' for housing me when I was homeless at age sixteen trusting your son's report of me.

Akinyele Oladeji, thank you for speaking well

of me to 'Mummy' and your lasting friendship ever since. You are more than a friend to me. You have become my blood brother.

'Uncle' Abiodun Daniel Farinde, you kept the ball rolling. Thank you for believing in me when I didn't see clearly. You were not only my teacher but you have become my father. Thank you for all you endured while I stayed in your house for all those years. May helpers of destiny not be far from you.

There are other teachers of my secondary school days that I must not but say thank you to: Mrs Shola Ojuola (Nee Ogunmokun) and Mrs Akinniyi. Thank you.

Mr And Mrs Bola Ajibike for your financial support and encouragement through those years in the University. May God remember you and fulfil your life.

Dr. Michael Olusanmi of Olajumoke Specialist Hospital, Iwo road, Ibadan, Nigeria. Out of sight is not out of mind! How can I ever forget your goodwill? You are always in my mind. May God's grace and peace be multiplied to you and your seeds abundantly.

I will but make mention of you, my father-in-the Lord, Pastor Matthew Ashimolowo, for those years of tutelage for the ministry. They were tough years but they were worth it! Thank you for all your fatherly care.

Last but not the least, my other father-in-the-Lord, Apostle Alfred T B Williams, thank you for your enduring love and care. Your teachings have brought a lot of refreshing to my soul.

The book has been long overdue but here it is at last. This is for all of you.

ACKNOWLEDGEMENTS

Many thanks go to all the people who have made writing this book project a success: Mr Anthony Adjarhore for the initial proof-reading. Thank you for the hours you spent combing through the book. Mr Abiola Bamigbade for double cheking the already checked.

Mr Babatunde Agoro, thank you for the beautiful attempts on the Cover design.

Yet again, Ms Doreen Munemo for all the efforts in spotting the little errors. Mr & Mrs Joe and Hikmot Ademosu, you are a delight to work with. Thank you for understanding many times the 'state of the affairs of the nation'. You know wha' I mean?

PREFACE

There is a drive in each one of us to be recognised and acknowledged for importance and significance. It is an innate desire! Everyone of us is born with it. The degree of the drive may be different however, due to life experiences and environments of upbringing. Sometimes life's experiences cause others to suppress the drive while the same life experiences act as prime catalysts for others to seek an avenue to express it.

The difference comes because of the way individuals internalise life experiences. Some allow their experiences to make them better while others become bitter by them, thereby shortchanging themselves.

Opportunities to make a difference with our lives come to each one of us in different shapes and sizes. Some will recognise their opportunities while others are still waiting for theirs to come despite having gone through the same experiences. The problem with opportunities is that they do not always appear as you expect them to. They always come disguised as obstacles, disappointments, failures, setbacks etc. They don't always come fully processed. It takes an eager and hungry heart to see through the disguise and get to work with the opportunity.

Consider this saying from the Scripture,

"Thus says the LORD:
As the new wine is found in the cluster,
And one says, 'Do not destroy it,
For a blessing is in it,'
So will I do for My servants' sake,
That I may not destroy them all."
Isaiah 65:8(NKJV)

Two people prospect opportunities differently. Both desire a new wine, a new joy, a new life; a fulfilling life. Rather than God supplying a new wine, He gives a cluster of grapes. One says, "This is not what I desire." He eats it or angrily throws the cluster away. The other says, "Do not destroy it. For a blessing is in it." How do you get the blessing of new wine from the cluster? By processing it. So is the way of opportunities.

The perspective has to be right. The internalisation of the apparent setback or failure has to be right and this comes from knowing that God will not deny you of anything good that you desire. The better perspective comes from knowing that your life is a life of significance. No matter your experience, everything is preparing you to reign in life.

David was secretly anointed to replace Saul. God did not announce it to the whole land. Why not? First, to protect David since there was still an incumbent king on the throne. Second, that is the way God works! He anoints you secretly but promotes you publicly in His own timing. He wants you to reign over the land from the palace but does not introduce you to the palace as the next king, even though he has anointed you as the next king.

He introduces you to the king's palace through the back door. He by-passes the pomp and pageantry of public ordination to give you a footing in the palace court. There is a territory for you to dominate. There's a sphere of influence for you to govern. We all have the capacity to rule, exercise dominion and be counted for. Your sphere of influence is your domain. That is your land!

The position from which you exercise your influence is your palace. Are you in your palace? Have you left the determination of your domain to chances? Are you waiting for someone to lead you there? Are you putting your hope in someone to bring you to the palace? Do you think someone somewhere has the ability or power to mention your name in the palace court?

The question to ask is not, 'Who will God use to invite me to the palace?' but 'What will God use to introduce me to the palace?'. Some are looking for people in high places to bring them to the King's notice. Sometimes the problem with that is, 'If men set you up, God will upset you'.

There is a dimension to elevation and promotion that we have not critically considered.

[6] For exaltation comes neither from the east
Nor from the west nor from the south.
[7] But God is the Judge:
He puts down one,
And exalts another.
Psalm 75:6-7 (NKJV)

God specialises in networking. He is the Master Network Marketer. While we focus on the movers and shakers to do the job, He always has His own obscure man in place to do the connection but only after you have been qualified.

David got to the palace not because he had someone of importance introduce him to the king but because of what was observed in his life as the servant of Saul. The opportunity came not because David was ushered or recognised as the next king but because he was sent to solve a problem for the king. He came to the palace as a solution provider; a platform different to being a king. Yet he had already been anointed to replace the same king. There is a place for the anointing and there is a place for personal qualifications. One cannot replace the other. God takes care of the anointing business. The personal qualifications are your own responsibility.

This book looks at those qualifications that caused David to stand out among a variety of options as the only one able to pacify the king's madness.

It is the same set of qualifications that will bring you to the height of your career, the realisation of your dream and aspiration. Being promising is not enough! Being diligent with the promise upon your life by cultivating those qualifications will ensure your climb to the highest point possible on the ladder of success in your chosen career or path.

These principles will work anywhere you work them. They are not respecters of geographical locations. They are universal. These principles hold a force that is akin to a gravitational pull. Wherever you go, whatever situations you apply them to, they will work!

However, you are the one who must cultivate and develop them. It is not God's responsibility or anyone else's! You must become accountable and discharge it with consistency and a dogged tenacity.

Enjoy as you read.

1 Samuel 16:1-18 (NKJV)

16:[1] *Now the LORD said to Samuel, "How long will you mourn for Saul, seeing I have rejected him from reigning over Israel? Fill your horn with oil, and go; I am sending you to Jesse the Bethlehemite. For I have provided Myself a king among his sons."*

[2] *And Samuel said, "How can I go? If Saul hears it, he will kill me." And the LORD said, "Take a heifer with you, and say, 'I have come to sacrifice to the LORD.'*

[3] *Then invite Jesse to the sacrifice, and I will show you what you shall do; you shall anoint for Me the one I name to you."*

[4] *So Samuel did what the LORD said, and went to Bethlehem. And the elders of the town trembled at his coming, and said, "Do you come peaceably?"*

[5] *And he said, "Peaceably; I have come to sacrifice to the LORD. Sanctify yourselves, and come with me to the sacrifice." Then he consecrated Jesse and his sons, and invited them to the sacrifice.*

[6] So it was, when they came, that he looked at Eliab and said, "Surely the LORD'S anointed is before Him."

[7] But the LORD said to Samuel, "Do not look at his appearance or at the height of his stature, because I have refused him. For the Lord does not see as man sees; for man looks at the outward appearance, but the LORD looks at the heart."

[8] So Jesse called Abinadab, and made him pass before Samuel. And he said, "Neither has the LORD chosen this one."

[9] Then Jesse made Shammah pass by. And he said, "Neither has the LORD chosen this one."

[10] Thus Jesse made seven of his sons pass before Samuel. And Samuel said to Jesse, "The LORD has not chosen these."

[11] And Samuel said to Jesse, "Are all the young men here?" Then he said, "There remains yet the youngest, and there he is, keeping the sheep." And Samuel said to Jesse, "Send and bring him. For we will not sit down till he comes here."

[12] So he sent and brought him in. Now he was ruddy, with bright eyes, and good-looking. And the LORD said, "Arise, anoint him; for this is the one!"

[13] Then Samuel took the horn of oil and anointed him in the midst of his brothers; and the Spirit of the LORD came upon David from that day forward. So Samuel arose and went to Ramah.

[14] But the Spirit of the LORD departed from Saul, and a distressing spirit from the LORD troubled him.

[15] And Saul's servants said to him, "Surely, a distressing spirit from God is troubling you.

[16] Let our master now command your servants, who are before you, to seek out a man who is a skillful player on the harp; and it shall be that he will play it with his hand when the distressing spirit from God is upon you, and you shall be well."

[17] So Saul said to his servants, "Provide me now a man who can play well, and bring him to me."

[18] Then one of the servants answered and said, "Look, I have seen a son of Jesse the Bethlehemite, who is skillful in playing, a mighty man of valor, a man of war, prudent in speech, and a handsome person; and the LORD is with him."

CHAPTER ONE

Whose Son are you?

"Then one of the servants answered and said,
"Look, I have seen a son of Jesse the Bethlehe-
mite,"
1 Samuel 16:18 (NKJV)

Have you ever wondered, seeing a multitude
of people, 'Where have all these people come
from?' 'I wonder which house each one of them
has come from?' When I first started travelling
on the M1 (the motorway that connects broadly
the South East of England to the North East)
between London and Luton a few years back, I
used to be baffled seeing all the cars and trucks
heading to and fro on either side of the road,
and would think, 'Where is everybody going and
where are they coming from?'. Once I thought
aloud and my wife answered, 'Where are you
coming from and where are you going?'.
That put a stop to my bafflement.

The point is that regardless of how heavily pop-
ulated the earth is, each one of us has an origin
and a destination. I have never heard of anyone
drop out of the sky and become part of the human race. Such a weird entrance to earth only
happens in movies! Yes, aliens are not part of
the human race.

They are illegal immigrants! That's the reason they will never live among us. Forget ET! People will only ever cite their appearances. How true those sitings are can only be left to our imaginations!

Your roots

Every man that has ever lived on the surface of the earth was born by a woman, with the exception of Adam and Eve. Melchizedek can also be included in this group, if we go by Apostle Paul's account of his life.

Without father, without mother, without descent, having neither beginning of days, nor end of life; but made like unto the Son of God; abideth a priest continually.
Hebrews 7:3 (KJV)

Adam and Eve's case can be explained. They were the first. There were none before them. They were the models. They did not need to grow up physically but spiritually. Adam was God's own offspring.

*Which was the son of Enos, which was the son of
Seth, which was the son of Adam, which was the
son of God.*
Luke 3:38 (KJV)

Adam's creation necessitated that he only needed to look up to God spiritually. His root was in
God. His whole identity came from his Creator.
Everyone else after him derived their physical
identity from Adam, even his wife Eve.

Our identity is anchored in our roots. We take
pride in our roots. A people whose history is
lost is a people struggling with their identity
because their root is misplaced. No matter what
our roots look like, they are the springboard of
our lives. Roots are the core of feeling of importance and significance. When a man knows his
roots he has a sense of belonging. The feeling of
belonging may not necessarily follow a sense of
belonging except the roots affirm the offspring.
Jesus at one time asked His disciples, 'Who do
men say that I, the Son of man, am?'.

There came multiple answers to the one question, 'Some say John the Baptist, some Elijah,
and others Jeremiah or one of the prophets'. Jesus rephrased His question, 'But who do you say

that I am?' Peter, aided by the Holy Spirit, replied 'You are the Christ, the Son of the living God'.

And Simon Peter answered and said, Thou art the Christ, the Son of the living God.
Matthew 16:16 (KJV)

The motivation behind Jesus' question is not that He did not know His roots and so needed help from others to ascertain His identity. Rather, He wanted His disciples, those who matter to Him the most in His circle of relationships, to know His roots and therefore locate His identity. If the Son of God desired to show His pedigree, how much more would you need to identify your roots?

Physical roots

No one decides their roots. Each one of us has to discover our physical roots. Things do happen sometimes that deny a man from identifying his roots. It may be due to rape, recklessness of life-style, or a one night-stand scenario that leads to the birth of a baby. Such a person only gets to know the mother and not the father.

But fathers are the root. Fathers determine the gender and fathers determine the identity.

Physical roots, as important as they are, are not more important than spiritual roots. Did you notice in the above scenario that Jesus, though He recognised His physical roots and connection, 'Who do men say that I, the Son of man, am?' He was much more concerned about His spiritual roots?

Granted, knowing your physical roots does help. It helps you to: receive affirmation of your identity, reveals your limitations, exposes your possibilities, fuels your sense of pride and gives you a sense of belonging. But understanding your spiritual roots does so much more.

Spiritual roots

Becoming connected to your spiritual roots does much more than all the benefits of knowing your physical roots. It provides a perspective to your life, your mission, your purpose, your destiny; the reason for being on earth. Jesus went beyond His physical affiliation to His spiritual origin to expose it as the springboard for His earthly mission. His physical parents did not determine His spiritual origin, they were His physical origin. His heavenly Father pre-determined His destination. There are no limitations to your spiritual roots if you locate them in God. There are no weaknesses in God. Therefore the possibilities are endless.

If you are not yet connected to your spiritual roots, it is easy and straightforward to do so. Jesus is the way to the Father of all spirits:

Furthermore we have had fathers of our flesh which corrected us, and we gave them reverence: shall we not much rather be in subjection unto the Father of spirits, and live?
Hebrews 12:9 (KJV)

Jesus said, 'I am the Way, the Truth and the Life. No one comes to the Father except through Me' Turn to page 130 of this book and pray the simple prayer that will connect you back to your spiritual roots. When? Now!

David was introduced to the palace first because his physical roots were identified but he himself knew better. He looked beyond his physical roots for affirmation:

*'When my father and my mother forsake me.
Then the Lord will take care of me'*
Psalm 27:10 (KJV)

Mentors

Though father and mother may sometimes not
provide the affirmation you need to develop
proper self-esteem, mentors and coaches are al-
ternative roots to affirm your person. Mentors
take the place of parents to supply whatever is
lacking in our development. They are God-sent.
In fact, the name, 'mentor' derives from Greek
mythology. In Homer's *Odyssey*, Mentor was the
trusted guardian the Greek warrior, Odyssey,
left his son, Telemachus, with when he was going to the Trojan war. The war lasted ten years
and it took another ten years for Odyssey to re-
turn home. By the time he got back home, he
realised that Telemachus had been nurtured to
become a man by Mentor.

How do you find a mentor? Mentors are every-
where. They are those whom you feel drawn and
attracted to because you admire certain qualities in them. They cannot take the place of your
father, though they fulfil the fatherly role to an

extent. They are the ones you dream of becoming like. They inspire, challenge and encourage you. They are the ones you feel comfortable to approach to help you develop in certain areas of your life.

You will be attracted to certain mentors for specific areas of development. Mentors are often times busy people. So you will need to learn to pursue them until you are impacted with what you desire to get from them. The proof of your pursuit is your desire. Many mentors will create time out of no time for you because you have been diligent to pursue them. The initiative lies with you. At the first meeting with your prospective mentor you need to be able to clarify and state exactly what it is you desire to get from the relationship and agree on how long it will take to achieve your objective.

Be careful you are choosing a mentor because of his character. On the other hand, it is his personality that may first endear you to him. But upon close contact, if what you see is not desirable with regards to his character, it's time you found another one.

With prayer for direction and Godly wisdom, the Lord will bring to your life those who will mark your life positively.

Dead Men Can Nurture You

The first time I heard the phrase, 'Dead men can mentor you.' I was curious to know how, until it was explained that it is made possible through the books written by those who are no longer with us. I have found out in my own life that at certain times in my spiritual walk I feel drawn to certain categories of books and I do not take my teeth out off them until I have satisfied my spirit's desires.

In the initial period of my Christian walk, Kenneth Hagin's books were all I wanted to get and read. In fact, I so much desired not only to read his books but to attend Rhema Bible Training Centre, Tulsa, Oklahoma, that my desire induced a dream where I received an academic scholarship from him. It was about twenty-four-years ago and in reality it never materialised. I still read his books today but not with the same ferocity that once caused me to devour them.

Then came another time that it was mainly the area of family life I desired to know and study. I guess this happened because nothing adequately prepared me for marriage. I wish I had been told that there is more to marriage than someone bearing your name. It is an awesome responsibility. One's youthful sexual-drive cannot sustain it if there is no maturity of character. Obviously, as a twenty-four year old youth approaching twenty-five, I quickly wanted to escape the pull of sexual pressures and become one with my bride. The pull became much stronger when the romance of courtship happened over a six thousand mile separation over the span of two years.

Everything in me was crying to be married. I can not imagine what I would have done if I had not found a lifetime partner at that period of my life. The first key learning point for marriage for a man is leadership. The second key learning point is leadership. And, the third most important key is leadership. From my understanding, young men need to be mentored by older men not only when they are about to be married. They should also be mentored after they have been married, at least for the first few years of their married life.

The reason for this is obvious. The man is still a rookie in the department of 'home affairs'. Many a man gets disillusioned, easily and quickly, the moment he begins to have a protracted period of unresolved issues with his young and beautiful wife, and it begins to affect his peace of mind.

Let's face it a lot of young marriages go through an unbelievable display of immaturity from both parties. If hidden cameras were to be placed in the homes of a lot of young couples, and some older couples too, you would be surprised at what happens and what is said behind closed doors. A young husband approached me immediately after the Sunday service in our church. Perhaps the message motivated him to approach me or maybe he felt that he needed to talk to me as his pastor; as it is rare for a man to be the first to seek help when his marriage is going through a rough patch.

After narrating the problem he and his young wife were facing, he said what I always dread to hear has happened in a marriage before it comes to the pastor – talking to the parents. In my opinion, the church should be the first to know of any difficulties a marriage is experiencing, if both parties are members of a church, with the sole aim of resolving the issues without any vested interest other than restoring peace to the home. This should be done to shield the marriage from unnecessary exposure to the risks of favouritism and unfair comments and involvement from in-laws. However my fear was allayed when the young man recounted his father's statements and advice to me. It became obvious that the young man's father was actually mentoring his son in the art of leading his family. In fact, I was further impressed when he said that his father particularly instructed him not to tell his mum of the marital ordeal so as to shield his wife from his mum's possible castigation of her. That is what I call mentoring in the art of leadership in the home front from an older man to a younger man.

It is even more admirable if it comes from the young man's father himself. We have a problem on our hands in our current generation. A lot of young men are going into marriage today without having seen their own fathers lead the family actively or they have been raised by their mother alone all their lives and get married to independent, career minded women who have already seen their own mothers survive years of abandonment from their fathers too.

It is a panacea for trouble in the home if there is no re-training of the minds to the biblical way. The solution is more than providing sessions of pre-marital counselling. There is need for providing an on-going class attendance that re-examines the issues addressed in pre-marital counselling sessions. This class attendance will be synonymous to providing after-sale service once the sale has been closed. If you consider the wedding as the closing of the deal, which product would best require this after-sale service above the rest other than marriage itself? Marriage mentors are the best substitutes in the absence of honourable fathers who cannot mentor their sons. Even, in cases where mentors are not forthcoming, books written by reputable men both living and dead can mentor whoever is preparing himself for life's opportunities.

David was recognised as the son of Jesse. Jesse was his father. Jesse was his root. Jesse was his covering. He had been nurtured and disciplined by Jesse. David had been submissive to his father's authority so he could be relied on to submit to the king's authority and consequentially could be relied upon to provide authority to others as well, if occasion demanded it.

The question of authority

In fact the question, 'Whose son are you?' begs for the answer of revealing whose authority you operate under or whose voice we can identify you with. I know today's generation doesn't like hearing about authority and submission. Yet there can be no proper functioning in life without order, authority and submission. Someone must lead in any given situation whilst someone else must follow. The role can be entirely reversed in another situation. It is dangerous to commit leadership to a person who has never learnt to submit to somebody else's authority. The grace to lead others flows from the heart that has been humbled in submission to another higher authority. David's recognition as the son of Jesse flows from the acknowledgement that he has been under the authority of his father. Exploring this further you will not be surprised to find occasions of his submission to his father's authority in his life events.

There is no better way to illustrate David's heart of submission to his father's authority than him being left alone to shepherd the family's flock in the backwoods of Bethlehem on the day Prophet Samuel visited the household to anoint him as King Saul's successor. There is no denying the fact that Jesse knew beforehand that Samuel would be paying a priestly visit to the family because all other sons were present to hospitably receive him except David. David could have been told that it was a men's affair and he being only a boy need not show his face. So he obeyed.

1 Samuel 16:1-13 (KJV)
And the Lord said unto Samuel, How long wilt thou mourn for Saul, seeing I have rejected him from reigning over Israel? fill thine horn with oil, and go, I will send thee to Jesse the Bethlehemite: for I have provided me a king among his sons. [2] And Samuel said, How can I go? if Saul hear it, he will kill me. And the Lord said, Take an heifer with thee, and say, I am come to sacrifice to the Lord.

[3] And call Jesse to the sacrifice, and I will shew thee what thou shalt do: and thou shalt anoint unto me him whom I name unto thee. [4] And Samuel did that which the Lord spake, and came to Bethlehem. And the elders of the town trembled at his coming, and said, Comest thou peaceably? [5] And he said, Peaceably: I am come to sacrifice unto the Lord: sanctify yourselves, and come with me to the sacrifice.

And he sanctified Jesse and his sons, and called them to the sacrifice.

[6] And it came to pass, when they were come, that he looked on Eliab, and said, Surely the Lord's anointed is before him. [7] But the Lord said unto Samuel, Look not on his countenance, or on the height of his stature; because I have refused him: for the Lord seeth not as man seeth; for man looketh on the outward appearance, but the Lord looketh on the heart. [8] Then Jesse called Abinadab, and made him pass before Samuel. And he said, Neither hath the Lord chosen this.

[9] Then Jesse made Shammah to pass by. And he said, Neither hath the Lord chosen this. [10] Again, Jesse made seven of his sons to pass before Samuel. And Samuel said unto Jesse, The Lord hath not chosen these. [11] And Samuel said unto Jesse, Are here all thy children? And he said, There remaineth yet the youngest, and, behold, he keepeth the sheep. And Samuel said unto Jesse, Send and fetch him: for we will not sit down till he come hither.

[12] And he sent, and brought him in. Now he was ruddy, and withal of a beautiful countenance, and goodly to look to. And the Lord said, Arise,

anoint him: for this is he. [13] Then Samuel took the horn of oil, and anointed him in the midst of his brethren: and the Spirit of the Lord came upon David from that day forward. So Samuel rose up, and went to Ramah.

Timothy's example

The truth of the argument of the verses in 1 Samuel 16 are further exemplified through the life of Timothy, the spiritual son of Apostle Paul. Even in our contemporary world you will hardly find a successful person, across any industry mentionable, that will not attest to being marked for difference by a father or a mentor, be it by spiritual or blood connection, who has played a significant role in their journey of success.

Timothy was no different. If it were not for Paul, we would never have heard of Timothy. If not for the relationship between him and Paul, he could have become one of those names that appeared in the pages of the Scriptures once and then disappeared. Timothy was one of three people in the New Testament Paul addressed as 'my son'. The other two were Titus and Onesimus.

Paul's letters to Timothy are today called Pastoral letters. But that was not Paul's intended name for them when he was penning them. They were meant to be encouraging personal letters of a father to his son as he discharged duties assigned to him by his father. They were letters of the heart of a father who was interested in his son's success.

The point must not be overlooked: the affirmation the father supplies, is the shoulder the son stands on to leap into the future.

Jesus is the Ultimate Standard

Jesus was affirmed publicly by His heavenly Father twice in the New Testament. Why would the Son of God who is also God within the Godhead need to be affirmed by another member of the Godhead? The truth of the matter is that Jesus, in his earthly ministry, was not a member of the Godhead. He was a member of humanity who needed encouragement from His father just like anybody else. The affirmation came at crucial stages in Jesus' life: first, at the assumption of ministry and secondly, later at the significant curve of change in His ministry. If you have ever had to start a ministry or business or a project on your own before, you will understand that what you must not have in shortage at the beginning of such an endeavour is encouragement or affirmation whilst you find your footing.

Matthew 3:16-17 (KJV)

And Jesus, when he was baptized, went up straightway out of the water: and, lo, the heavens were opened unto him, and he saw the Spirit of God descending like a dove, and lighting upon him: [17] And lo a voice from heaven, saying, This is my beloved Son, in whom I am well pleased.

Luke 9:28-35 (KJV)

And it came to pass about an eight days after these sayings, he took Peter and John and James, and went up into a mountain to pray. [29] And as he prayed, the fashion of his countenance was altered, and his raiment was white and glistering. [30] And, behold, there talked with him two men, which were Moses and Elias: [31] Who appeared in glory, and spake of his decease which he should accomplish at Jerusalem. [32] But Peter and they that were with him were heavy with sleep: and when they were awake, they saw his glory, and the two men that stood with him. [33] And it came to pass, as they departed from him, Peter said unto Jesus, Master, it is good for us to be here: and let us make three tabernacles; one for thee, and one for Moses, and one for Elias: not knowing what he said. [34] While he thus spake, there came a cloud, and overshadowed them: and they feared as they entered into the cloud. [35] And there came a voice out of the cloud, saying, This is my beloved Son: hear him.

The gospel of Luke is the only book of the synoptic gospels that hints as to the content of discussion among Moses, Elias and Jesus, that warranted the affirmation from His Father. I do not know of any man who would be reminded of imminent death, especially of a death he did not deserve, that would not require encouragement or affirmation. And the best affirmation could only come from the One to whom the death signified total obedience to His will.

If you are on your way to the palace, we must be able to trace your father. It is the order of God. Yes, many biological fathers have failed in their role but God never leaves anyone without a witness to His faithfulness. Whose influence has moulded you? Whose shadow has been your covering while God prepared you for the palace?

2 Timothy 2:1-2 (KJV)
Thou therefore, my son, be strong in the grace
that is in Christ Jesus. [2] And the things that
thou hast heard of me among many witnesses,
the same commit thou to faithful men, who shall
be able to teach others also.

The Uzz factor of personal development

'The *Uzz factor*' actually stands for '*The Uzziah
factor*' in any personal development. It is a factor that recognises the contribution of others in
any personal achievement.

The truth of the matter is that no one is an is-
land. You did not arrive by yourself. The story of
a self-made man is a myth. Someone somewhere
somehow along the way contributed to your get-
ting here. You rode on somebody's shoulder to
get here. Who is it? Yes, sometimes our pride
does not allow us to acknowledge those who
washed our diapers when we did not even know
our left from our right. We have been deceived
too long by the story of 'The Lone Ranger' who
needed no one to help him achieve an incredible
result. Even then, Mr Lone Ranger had a Toto.

Some time ago I was approached by a long time family friend, who had just started to produce a Christian Men's magazine called *Brothers*, to contribute a write-up for a regular column in the magazine.

After a period of praying and tossing with the idea of what to start with, since it was going to be a regular feature of the magazine, it was impressed upon my heart to re-examine a passage of Scriptures I had recently used at the Prayer meeting of a church in London. The whole article is printed below starting with the focus passage:

2 Chronicles 26:1-9 (KJV)

[26:1] Then all the people of Judah took Uzziah, who was sixteen years old, and made him king in the room of his father Amaziah. [2] He built Eloth, and restored it to Judah, after that the king slept with his fathers.[3] Sixteen years old was Uzziah when he began to reign, and he reigned fifty and two years in Jerusalem. His mother's name also was Jecoliah of Jerusalem. [4] And he did that which was right in the sight of the LORD, according to all that his father Amaziah did. [5] And he sought God in the days of Zechariah, who had understanding in the visions

of God: and as long as he sought the LORD, God made him to prosper.[6] And he went forth and warred against the Philistines, and brake down the wall of Gath, and the wall of Jabneh, and the wall of Ashdod, and built cities about Ashdod, and among the Philistines.[7] And God helped him against the Philistines, and against the Arabians that dwelt in Gur-baal, and the Mehunims. [8] And the Ammonites gave gifts to Uzziah: and his name spread abroad even to the entering in of Egypt; for he strengthened himself exceedingly. [9]Moreover Uzziah built towers in Jerusalem at the corner gate, and at the valley gate, and at the turning of the wall, and fortified them.

The potential for your development is unlimited. Without your development though there is no room for dominion. Dominating is what you are doing when you are successful and prospering. The above passage introduces to us the right definition of prosperity. Prosperity is not about what you have managed to amass for yourself. It is not about what you are able to flaunt to announce your arrival or how much you have stockpiled for your personal enjoyment. It is simple really. It is what you are able to do within your available resources to positively affect the lives of others. This is achievement. This is real success. This is the true definition of prosperity. *Spending your life for the betterment of others!* Expending your life for social or community transformation. This is where history recognises you because you have made your mark on the rock of time, not on the soil of time. Those who make their mark on the soil have it erased by the following generation. However, when it is etched on the rock of time no one can erase it. It's forever!

The Uzz factor in your personal achievement is actually a crucial factor in your success equation as it is glimpsed from the life of Uzziah, the king of Judah, who reigned from about 701 BC to 649 BC, and made a difference in his lifetime. Unfortunately though, he's much remembered for his shameful end rather than his brilliant start. That is another lesson entirely for you in *U Development Unlimited.*

It is important to note that people don't bother to remember your beginning they are only interested in your finishing. Life itself doesn't really care how you were packaged for the start of the race, it only etches in its memory how you finished the race. The old adage says, ' *The bad that men do is carved out in solid; the good they do is written on water'.* Continuity is the name of the race. Start well; finish well. Start bad, but change along the way, and finish well. Life will forgive your beginning but it rarely forgets your end. Uzziah *'sought God in the days of Zechariah, who had understanding in the visions of God: and as long as he sought the LORD, God made him to prosper.'*

This is the unchanging factor in your success equation. What do you mean? I mean he sought God. Seeking God to make a difference is the beginning, the first composite part of the factor. Greatness is not transferable. It is custom made. It is tailor-made because seeking God is not transferable. Yes, it can be observed and emulated. But it always has to be worked out through personal involvement and accepting responsibility. Uzziah sought the Lord for himself. And Zechariah sought the Lord for himself.

Zechariah neither sought the Lord for Uzziah nor did Uzziah seek the Lord for Zechariah. However, there was a meeting point for both of them. Uzziah received visions from the Lord while Zechariah assumed an understanding of their interpretations from the Lord.

The summary of the factor is this: Remember, Uzziah was only sixteen when he began to reign in Judah. In our contemporary language, he was a teenager. Can you imagine a teenager ruling Britain today? Can you imagine our Prime Minister being a teenager? That is the picture of Uzziah with all the imaginations you can conjure up similar to our present day teenagers. But the difference between him and today's teenagers, however, is that he had Zechariah to mentor him. He had Zechariah to encourage him in his new position as king over the nation. He was not self-assured with the new position.

He realised that he needed someone to watch over him in the governance of the state. He had advisers surrounding him but notably he had a spiritual adviser in the person of Zechariah who stood out among his many advisers. He had a role model to teach him his role.

During one of his sessions at the Uncommon Leaders Summit organised by a church in Lagos, Nigeria, Bishop David Oyedepo emphasised, 'You cannot play your role without a role model.' In fact, he shared that he studied 39 biographies of people whom he admired in ministry before he started his own, *The Living Faith Ministries*.

So it is with every achiever, they channel past successes to navigate their own future.

Role models have been to where you are going. They have trodden the path you are about to begin. They have run the race you are about to start. Each race is unique yet there are similar points of experience along the way. Why reinvent the wheel when you can accelerate with an old one? Who are your role models in life? What do you know about them? What strategies have you identified in their lives that can sharpen your strengths and caution your weaknesses?

God meant for you to stand on the shoulders of those who made a difference in past generations to leap into the future. On whose shoulders are you standing? How can you see clearly into the future when you don't have the advantage of height? Yes, you must seek the Lord for yourself but you must have a human agent through whom you can look at the past and the future by standing on their shoulders.

As long as you seek the Lord, without neglecting His agents who cry with the voice of experience you shall prosper. History would write you in its annals. If you seek the Lord and cry for exemplified and practical wisdom He will send you human agents. In fact, 'Dead men can mentor you through their books', writes John Maxwell. So there is no excuse for you in this Information Age. The information you need on any notable achiever of the past and the present is available to you at the click of a button. What are you doing? Set the ball rolling and change your generation for the better.

Have you received a vision from the Lord for your life? Who is your cheerleader? Who nurtures you as you nurture the dream? Who encourages you as you push back the horizon ahead of you? Who speaks to your fear and feeds your boldness? A wise man once said, 'Encouragement is the oxygen of the soul.' So whose words of encouragement are keeping you going and reassuring your steps? Zechariah understood the visions of God. Who understands your visions? Remember, he is not your team player. He is your cheerleader. He is outside of your team but he has your best interests at heart.

Perhaps, you think you don't need one. Are you saying you don't need one because you are not a teenager? You have come of age now. You are in your 20's, 30's or even your 40's. If you are ever going to make a mark, of necessity, surely you need one. 'One is too small a number to achieve significance', wrote John Maxwell in his book, *The 17 Laws of Teamwork*. Work 'the Uzz factor in personal achievement' and it will work for you.

CHAPTER TWO

Skillfull in playing

...who is skillful in playing,..."
1 Samuel 16:18 (NKJV)

It still beats my imagination to accept that at
the age of fifteen David had become known as a
skilful harp player in the palace of Saul. On the
other hand, the possibility of his fame to have
travelled far to the ears of those in the palace at
such a tender age could not have been difficult
really when you consider, in our contemporary
world, the likes of Venus and Serena Williams,
the ace lawn tennis players, who broke through
to the limelight in the tennis world while in their
teens. The pace their father took them through
was amazing.

Though we did not read how Jesse coached David on how to play the harp, he must have honed
his skills while tendering the sheep in the graz-
ing pasture of Bethlehem by himself. If this was
not so, how would you have explained how his
father forgot to include him in the line up for
Prophet Samuel when he came calling to ordain
one of his sons for kingship. Definitely, he must
have had a flair for music. But he did not just
rely on his natural disposition for music, the
'sweet psalmist of Israel' went a step higher by
sharpening what he had a flair for.

Skills are not developed overnight. It takes a great deal of consistency and patience to become proficient in anything worthwhile.

Ain't no skills by osmosis

Osmosis is a scientific word used commonly in the study of Biology. It describes the process of sharing food by two species or living objects placed side by side without physical contact. This can easily by achieved by species that are not highly developed and structured like human beings as the story is different among us created in the image of God.

There is a deception at large among believers who think that purely by the laying on of hands skills that have taken painful years of practice and honing, by a public figure in ministry, can easily be transferred. Skills cannot merely be transferred by osmosis. They have to be learned and earned. If you are not ready to learn it, you are not ready to earn it. Recently I read in one of Rick Joyner's books, 'A Prophetic Vision for the 21st Century', of instances where individuals had asked for prayers from him for an impartation of skills to write books in the same fashion as he does. I suppose that is laziness taken to the extreme or covetousness smothered with religiosity. Whichever you call it, skills have to be earned through tears and sweat. Joyner tells of the thousands of books he had to read to get to where he is today as a writer.

It takes skill to write a book for public consumption! It takes a great deal of skill to be a prolific writer as Rick Joyner or any other great writer known in the Body of Christ. What we often see and admire of these writers are the products of sweat and tears even if the books are transcribed from a collection of their messages. Transcribed messages are not always repeated verbatim; they have to be edited and restructured in a way that makes sense to potential readers.

If many of these great writers could tell the stories of what it took them to finish a whole book, or their transcriptions for that matter, then you would appreciate the saying that 'Behind the glory there is a story' of pain and labour, burning the midnight oil and what have you!

Discover Your Flair

It goes back to saying that David discovered his flair for composing music and playing the harp early enough to hone them. Skills can be developed in any area of life you desire. But it is much easier to develop skills in areas you already have a natural flair for. When the Scriptures encourage parents or guardians to *'Train up a child in the way he should go: and when he is old, he will not depart from it'* (Prov.22:6), oftentimes, it has been understood to mean 'give a child a moral training and he will not depart from it'. The understanding of that verse becomes limiting if that is all there is to it. I prefer the way the Amplified version puts it: *'Train up a child in the way he should go [and in keeping with his individual gift or bent], and when he is old he will not depart from it'*.

Children show their natural flair at the very early stages of their growing years. Some parents are wise enough to notice and begin to direct their child according to their gifts and bents. Some parents have a pre-conceived idea of what they want their child to be. As a result they fail to observe and acknowledge the natural gifts but instead train their child according to their own expectations rather than the child's bent. This may cause the child to become frustrated later on in life.

It is very common in the African culture I was raised in. It is not strange to see a young person who has spent years pursuing a particular line of education, even up to the university level, switch to a completely different field after their first degree graduation. Why? The story always reveals that the first degree pursued was just to please Dad or Mum. Now that the young man or woman has gained freedom from the overbearing influence of Dad or Mum he or she can then pursue what he or she always wanted. What a waste of time and energy!

While this kind of story ends well for a few who switched over early enough, there are millions who do not have enough confidence or boldness to start all over again because they do not want to go against their father or mother's wishes or it is too big a price to start afresh after many wasted years. Such people die in the shadows of their parents wish. They never find out what it is to be original. It can be quite frustrating. And this, oftentimes, slips over to other areas of life and affects them negatively.

What are you naturally good at? What are your earliest recollections of your daydreams? That is a pointer to your flair. Daydreams are different to wishful thinking of childhood. Daydreams are synonymous to patterns of desires and actions you have followed over the years and come to you with ease whereas wishful thinking passes away with different stages of your growing years.

When our son was three going on four, he always wanted to be a fireman. At another stage he wanted to be a policeman. However, consistently from the first time we started reading bedtime storybooks to him, he could pick up the storybooks and repeat them verbatim to us without being able to recognise the words of the storybook in another context. But with the pictures in the storybook he could scale over the book in record time.

And he has maintained this interest in book reading up until now. The first time he wrote a fictitious story as homework from school, I almost doubted it was original. He has consistently excelled in English and literary subjects. At any point in time he is always with a reading book, storybook in particular. Seeing this interest in reading storybooks gears me to buy voluminous books for him and challenge him to read and summarise them for me with occasional rewards, of course.

Bookish or Bookworm

My wife has this theory of the difference between being bookish and being a bookworm. Her theory goes like this: Bookish people are people who like to collect books and decorate their studies with them but they are not committed to reading them. While bookworms are those who read anything and everything they lay their hands on. She goes further with her theory: bookish people tend to be tidy with their books while bookworms are scatter-brains when it comes to organising their collections.

In any case, it is good to develop a love for book reading whether you have a flair for it or not. Books will definitely make you excel in your chosen field. Readers become leaders. The edge of any leadership is sharpened by the knowledge gleaned from books written by those ahead of the leaders.

Is there any insight from the Bible to see if David had a lifestyle of reading that could have honed his life skills? Yes, the following provides an interesting glimpse to his love for the Torah.

Psalm 1:2 (KJV)
But his delight is in the law of the Lord; and in his law doth he meditate day and night.

Psalm 19:7 (KJV)
The law of the Lord is perfect, converting the soul: the testimony of the Lord is sure, making wise the simple.

Psalm 40:8 (KJV)
I delight to do thy will, O my God: yea, thy law is within my heart.

Psalm 78:5 (KJV)
For he established a testimony in Jacob, and appointed a law in Israel, which he commanded our fathers, that they should make them known to their children:

Psalm 94:12 (KJV)
Blessed is the man whom thou chastenest, O Lord, and teachest him out of thy law;

Psalm 119:18 (KJV)

Open thou mine eyes, that I may behold wondrous things out of thy law.

Psalm 119:34 (KJV)

Give me understanding, and I shall keep thy law; yea, I shall observe it with my whole heart.

Psalm 119:44 (KJV)

So shall I keep thy law continually for ever and ever.

Psalm 119:51 (KJV)

The proud have had me greatly in derision: yet have I not declined from thy law.

Psalm 119:55 (KJV)

I have remembered thy name, O Lord, in the night, and have kept thy law.

Psalm 119:70 (KJV)

Their heart is as fat as grease; but I delight in thy law.

Psalm 119:72 (KJV)

The law of thy mouth is better unto me than thousands of gold and silver.

Psalm 119:77 (KJV)
Let thy tender mercies come unto me, that I may live: for thy law is my delight.

Psalm 119:92 (KJV)
Unless thy law had been my delights, I should then have perished in mine affliction.

Psalm 119:97 (KJV)
O how love I thy law! it is my meditation all the day.

Psalm 119:109 (KJV)
My soul is continually in my hand: yet do I not forget thy law.

Psalm 119:113 (KJV)
I hate vain thoughts: but thy law do I love.

Psalm 119:163 (KJV)
I hate and abhor lying: but thy law do I love.

Psalm 119:165 (KJV)
Great peace have they which love thy law: and nothing shall offend them.

Psalm 119:174 (KJV)
I have longed for thy salvation, O Lord; and thy law is my delight.

The relationship of David to God's Word is highlighted in Psalm 119 more than any other chapter in the Bible. I encourage you to read the whole chapter and be encouraged and inspired by the intimacy of the sweet Psalmist of Israel with God's Word. There seems to be a correlation between David's love for the Torah and his ability to write great songs, today known as the Psalms. There also seems to be a prophetic edge to the writing of the many Psalms penned by David. Definitely, a divine inspiration to write the Psalms flowed from the reading of the Torah with accompanied melody from his harp which filtered through to the palace of Saul.

Born with Skills?

It is erroneous to think that any man is born with skills. No man is born with any skill. We were born with certain reflexes that later developed to skills. All skills are learnt here on this earth. The degree to which individuals develop their talents, gifts and bents determine how skilful they will be. The choice lies with the individual. You can become the best in your chosen field or you can become the least recognised.

The difference between a mediocre and a skilful person in any area of discipline is the self-mastery exerted by individuals to their craft. Mediocre people put minimal effort to their work; skilful persons exert themselves to be their best. Solomon observed the way of a lazy man and a diligent man in different settings and concluded: first, the difference starts with their individual attitude.

Proverbs 12:27 (KJV)
The slothful man roasteth not that which he took in hunting: but the substance of a diligent man is precious.

It has been said that a man's attitude will determine his altitude. Learning to be thorough with whatever they do is an attitude that the diligent have developed. They go over their finished work to see if they have remembered to dot their i's and cross their t's. They do not leave anything to chance. In fact they go beyond the call of duty to the point of sacrifice, thereby pushing the boundaries of mediocrity to the point of excellence. The project at hand might well be his last project but he's going to give it his best shot anyway. He could not care whether it belonged to him or not, since he has charge of it, he might as well do it as if it belonged to him.

On the other hand, the slothful man gives his minimal effort to the work at hand. He is a good starter but a bad finisher. He gets easily discouraged and overwhelmed by the demands of excellence. He cannot be bothered about whose ox is gored. The language of examining his work again and again to see how he could do better is foreign to him. He fails to realise that his work is his signature.

Secondly, King Solomon observed the life of a slothful man and receives instructions for living:

Proverbs 22:13 (KJV)
The slothful man saith, There is a lion without, I shall be slain in the streets.

Years ago I read a book which perfectly depicts the attitude of the slothful man here. A lazy man is giving excuses for his inactivity hence his failure to develop his skills. The book I read pointed out that those who always give excuses for their failure suffer from a disease called 'excusitis'. Now, do you notice that the lazy man's excuse is an external one whereas his problem stems from the inside of himself?

I have used this verse to minister on a Sunday service before and one of the things I notice is the defeatist attitude that is characteristic of a lazy man. If there was ever a lion in the street, why couldn't the lazy man join other men to kill the beast? Lastly, another observation of King Solomon in the life of a lazy man in contrast with a skilful or diligent man depicts a lot of activity but no progress

Proverbs 26:14 (KJV)
[14] As the door turneth upon his hinges, so doth the slothful upon his bed.

Each time a door turns upon its hinges it covers a distance in an arc form. In this way depending on how many times the door moves upon its hinges as people open and close it, the door can cover a measurable distance, say a mile. Yet, it remains on the same spot.

The wisdom here is that a lazy man may always be busy but there is no productivity; no effectiveness. This suggests that it is not enough to be busy doing things when there is nothing to show for it. If you were ever busy doing the same thing for a considerable number of years without any improvement on the bottom-line then that is a form of laziness. A skilful man improves himself so he can be relevant to his days.

Staying in the same job for more than ten years without promotion and no refresher courses to attend in order to update one's skills is a form of laziness. It is allowing yourself to stay stuck in a rut.

In fact, ten years is too long to stay on one spot without a change for the better. The litmus test that Jesus gave in the New Testament is three years:

Luke 13:6-9 (KJV)
He spake also this parable; A certain man had a fig tree planted in his vineyard; and he came and sought fruit thereon, and found none. [7] Then said he unto the dresser of his vineyard, Behold, these three years I come seeking fruit on this fig tree, and find none: cut it down; why cumbereth it the ground? [8] And he answering said unto him, Lord, let it alone this year also, till I shall

dig about it, and dung it: [9] And if it bear fruit, well: and if not, then after that thou shalt cut it down.

There you have it. After three years of no productivity, it is time to 'dig and dung' yourself or your career lest you be cumbering the ground. The truth of the matter is, after a while of moving on its hinges the door becomes stiff and starts to creak loudly. At that point it needs to be lubricated. How much more would a person that has stayed in a rut with their job need to be refreshed and updated with new knowledge especially in this Information Age?

Staying in a job or career where nothing seems to be happening and nothing is moving forward is not God's best for any of His children. Even, being in a ministry where there is no freshness of the Holy Spirit and everything looks and tastes stale is a waste of time.

Proverbs 18:9 (KJV)
He also that is slothful in his work is brother to him that is a great waster.

Diligence *pays*; laziness *costs*

The analogy of life as a 'restaurant with a difference' has a measure of truth applicable to our
understanding of how diligence pays. A wise
man observed that in real life, if you go to a
restaurant, you are given a menu from which
you place your order. After eating well and be
satisfied, then you pay your bill. The restaurant
owner trusts you enough to pay your bill after
eating.

However, in the case of life endeavours, as a restaurant, life does not trust you enough to pay
after you have eaten. So life demands that you
pay before you eat in your endeavours. How
would you know when you have paid enough?
When you start enjoying the benefits of your
diligence! This altruism did not escape the observation of King Solomon either. The AMP Bible does a pertinent rendering of it:

Proverbs 22:29
Do you see a man diligent and skilful in his busi-
ness? He will stand before kings; he will not stand
before obscure men.

Today's English Version (TEV) gives it another interesting twist:

Proverbs 22:29 (TEV)
Show me someone who does a good job, and I will show you someone who is better than most and worthy of the company of kings.

'*Worthy of the company of kings*' was the case for David hence his royal invitation to the palace to placate an incumbent demonised king.

CHAPTER THREE

A mighty man
of valour

"...a mighty man of valor..."
1 Samuel 16:18 (NKJV)

Encarta Dictionary: English (U.K.) describes 'valour' as synonymous to 'courage; especially that shown in war or battle'. *Thesaurus: English (U.K.)* gives the following as exact synonyms for the word: courage, bravery, spirit, nerve, heroism, fearlessness, boldness, and gallantry. How could this description have fitted David since at this time he had not yet engaged Goliath in battle nor had he ever enrolled or been conscripted into any battle?

What would make anybody call a teenager 'a mighty man of valour' especially when his shirt is not bursting with bulging biceps? David once alluded to his stature as small through the Scriptures when he said, *'I am small and despised: yet do not I forget thy precepts.'* Psalm 119:141 (KJV) So it could not have been his physique that gave him away as a man of valour.

He was only fifteen when the servant introduced him as the solution provider to the king's problem. He definitely had neither been pumping steroids into his body, nor doing push-ups. If it was an angel who had called him a mighty man of valour, like the case of coward Gideon on his father's threshing floor, (Judges 6:11-14) then we would agree that he is 'calling those things that be not as though they were.'

And this statement from Saul's servant is not just faith words. They are backed by testimonies of exploits by David even at his tender age as they filtered through to the palace.

Brawn or Brain

So of certainty it is not a question of brawn. For Saul also attested to his appearance, '... *for thou art but a youth, and he a man of war from his youth.*' 1 Samuel 17:33 (KJV) This suggests he was youthful in his appearance. Since this is the case, the other option left for us to consider to account for this quality 'valour' in David's life would be that he was smart. If you are intelligent, you are considered smart. You might belong to Mensa International, a high-IQ society. But this was not David's case either; for no where was it suggested that he was smarter than his brethren.

In one instance in the Psalm he stated:

I have more understanding than all my teachers: for thy testimonies are my meditation. [100] I understand more than the ancients, because I keep thy precepts.
Psalm 119:99-100 (KJV)

So the key here is his love for the Torah. The access point to his exceptional understanding is spiritual; for the law, stated Apostle Paul in Romans 7:14, is spiritual. What David lacked in a high-IQ was most probably supplied in the richness of God's Word in his heart. It is not a question of his brain here but of his heart. His heart was steadfast in his God. He was aware that his mother had cast him upon the Lord from his youth:

But thou art he that took me out of the womb: thou didst make me hope when I was upon my mother's breasts. [10] I was cast upon thee from the womb: thou art my God from my mother's belly.
Psalm 22:9-10 KJV

This awareness gave him an early advantage that many later realised was possible: he had learned to trust God from childhood through a living relationship that could be the envy of most believers today. David was living beyond his age and time. He was living a New Testament life in an Old Testament time.

Wiser than his age

The richness of God's Word translated to David being wiser than his age. He himself affirmed the truth of this claim, *'Thou through thy commandments hast made me wiser than mine enemies: for they are ever with me.'* Psalm 119:98 (KJV)

The enormity of responsibility the young man assumed at an early age is another pointer to this truth coupled with the fact that the fall-out of his conquest over Goliath triggered an uncontrollable jealousy from Saul to the extent that the Bible says:

And David behaved himself wisely in all his ways; and the Lord was with him. [15] Wherefore when Saul saw that he behaved himself very wisely, he was afraid of him.
1 Samuel 18:14-15 (KJV)

You see, this wisdom did not only come on the occasion of his dealing with this demonic king. David had always been wise. How would you explain the fact that not once did he ever shoot his tongue out to Saul knowing fully well that he had already been anointed to replace him? He neither told him nor anybody in the palace saying, *'You watch out! I am going to be the next king after king Saul dies. He will soon die, you know. Prophet Samuel came to our house and anointed me the next king based on instructions from God. You think I'm lying? Ask Eliab, Abinadab or Shammah. I am not just here to play the harp. I'm here to take over!'*

He did not say any of those bragging statements teenagers are prone to utter. He knew the palace was going to be his eventually, yet he waited for a long time, until God gave it to him. Teenagers are not known, and some adults too, for accepting delayed gratification. Let's look at some of David's descendants, in later years, after the split of the kingdom, who could not delay their gratification and therefore assumed office with violence.

The likes of Jehu (2 Kings 9 & 10), Shallum (2 kings 15:10-13), Menahem (2 kings 15: 14-22),

Pekah (2 kings 15:25-29) and Hoshea (2 Kings 15:30- 17:4) all conspired against their predecessors. They did not have the wisdom of David who understood the law of God and honoured his predecessor.

Do you have similar insight to David who understood that the key to everything is through God and His Word? Do you have the courage to stand with God when all others stand against you? Do you have the boldness to remain steadfast in your resolve when it seems everyone else is against you?

Courage in the dark

All said and done I still do not think that this is sufficient to account for David's valour. Of necessity, the story of his exploits in killing the bear and the lion while looking after his father's flock is most appropriate to earn him the title: 'a man of valour'. You wouldn't call a teenager 'a man of valour' when he has not yet performed a heroic act, would you? An adult wouldn't hide it if he had killed a bear in the woods or a lion in the forest how much more a teenager? It takes enormous courage to face a lion when

he is strolling through the forest not to mention a hungry lion that has just found a lamb
to devour. David, with his own mouth gave the
account of his heroic performance against the
lion:

1 Samuel 17:34-36 (NKJV)
*But David said to Saul, "Your servant used to
keep his father's sheep, and when a lion or a bear
came and took a lamb out of the flock, [35] I went
out after it and struck it, and delivered the lamb
from its mouth; and when it arose against me, I
caught it by its beard, and struck and killed it.
[36] Your servant has killed both lion and bear;
and this uncircumcised Philistine will be like one
of them, seeing he has defied the armies of the
living God."*

Now, no one was watching when all this occurred. However, the news of these heroic actions would have spread like wildfire in Bethlehem. And the truth of it is only attested to
when an opportunity to repeat the act pre-
sented itself in the full glare of publicity. David did not baulk at the opportunity. Who
you are in private is always proven in public.
Champions are not made in public; they are
only recognised there. If you have been coura-

geous in the dark you will not shy away when the opportunity to do the same shows up in the public arena.

The reality of this axiom is that you should work on yourself when no one is watching so you will not be ashamed when the opportunity to prove yourself presents itself in public.

The rule of the game

The truth of the matter of life is that what you have not mastered in secret you cannot conquer in public. Athletes who compete in the public arena have a measure of confidence that they have done their home work well. If not, they expose themselves to ridicule and jeers. However, their best preparation may be another participant's worst performance. Nonetheless, when you have done your best in order to participate in a competition and yet without success, at least you can take consolation in the fact that you have done your best. Consistency is the rule of the game even when no one is applauding you. Keep at what you know to do best. Play the game according to the rules. The number one rule is that good preparation prevents poor performance. To fail to prepare is to prepare to fail when the opportunity presents itself for success.

When will you be successful? When you have adequately prepared yourself, all things being equal, the success will show up. The key is not to give up at what you are good at until your time to manifest shows up.

The price and the prize

The price of preparation is not always greater than the prize of recognition of success. But if you are not willing to pay the price of consistent discipline of preparation you may never be able to enjoy the pleasure of the prize of success. Be willing to do all that is necessary to take your place on the platform of success. Burn the midnight oil. Pay the price.

CHAPTER FOUR

A man of war

"...a man of war..." 1
Samuel 16:18 (NKJV)

Will to war

I would say that to call David a man of war prior to him fighting Goliath is a bit presumptuous. However, you don't need to have been involved in war before you are called a man of war if you have a will to war. A will to war is apparent if you are dogged, rugged, tenacious, do not easily give up and if you are impervious to the negative circumstances of life. A teenager who would not let go of his sheep in the mouth of a hungry lion definitely had a will to war though he had not been engaged in any war. What could be more of a war than to fight a lion and resist a grisly bear?

If you are going to succeed in life by your definition of success, you have to have a will to war. The world out there is a war! Someone once said that life does not give you what you ask of it but what you demand of it. To demand is to be insisting on what you want. If one method does not work you try another. If another doesn't deliver you move to the next one. In essence what this means is that you never give up; never to take no for an answer when you know that you are being denied what is your right to possess.

David could probably have let go of the lamb when it was caught between the teeth of the lion. After all, what is one lamb among many sheep? But the mentality of a man of war is that no one denies him of what is his. The attitude of attempting to try something bigger than yourself is also a characteristic of the will to war. If you have always been satisfied with the present harbour you will never know the joy of discovering a new harbour. What does it take to be better than where you are presently? What does it take to improve your life? What does it take to attain the dream that you have put on the shelf all this while?

The truth of life is that whatever you stretch to reach stretches you and never leaves you the same. Whatever you try to conquer opens up a new horizon you have not known before your conquest. It is all in the will to war. Even if you fail at your attempts, you are far better than the one who has not tried once. A wise man said, "Success in life is failure after failure without losing your enthusiasm."

What do you suppose is the whole essence of 'consultancy'? To my understanding, it is re-packaging failures in order to teach others not to fail in the same way and manner. I will not consult you if you have not tried and tested what you are offering me and have a testimony that it works. What others deem as failures, for you, have become stepping stones to higher grounds for others.

For a long time I have desired to be a writer but I have always been met with a mental block try-ing to see how to start and where to start. After many hours of reading other people's books, the possibilities began to open up that I could ex-press myself on the pages of a book without try-ing to be like any of the prolific writers I have admired for years. In fact, I also started to note the writers I do not want to be like because of their particular styles. There is nothing wrong with them; it's just that they don't inspire my creative writing ability.

Sticking with what you love to do until you decipher a better way to achieve your goal is a demonstration of your will to war. We prob-ably would not have heard about David and his exploits, if he had not had a will to war in the backwoods of Bethlehem against the bear and the lion, until the opportunity to war against Goliath came.

Do not take for granted all those secret opportunities confronting you and challenging you to flex your muscles. In other words, stop running from challenging circumstances. Face them, finish them and file them in your memory bank. You would need them for your imagination later. They are your résumé for your next promotion.

Battles versus War

Mind you, though life by itself, is a war it is broken into different battles. The culmination of the battles is what determines whether you have won the war or not. If you win more battles than you lose it is obvious you will win the war ultimately. Some battles are more strategic to the outcome of a war. Though you may have lost more battles, as long as you win the strategic ones the outcome will be favourable.

David asserted that God teaches his hands for war and fingers for battle (Psalm 144:1). He realised that life is broken into days but measured in years. During World War II, there were many battles fought. Some were lost by the Allies; some were worn by the Axis powers (the enemies). Ultimately, the war was won by the Allies after many other battles including the battle of Normandy.

Whatever contests for your destiny, has actually declared a war against you whether you want to fight or not. David became aware of his destiny from the moment Prophet Samuel anointed him in the midst of his brothers. Like it or not, that began his introduction into a life of open battles of which he could not afford to lose the war. Maybe that was why he penned the famous verse of Psalm 23:

Psalm 23:5 (NKJV)
You prepare a table before me in the presence of my enemies; You anoint my head with oil;
My cup runs over.

The prepared table of the Lord is not an empty table. Of a truth it had to have been full of different provisions but the problem is that the Lord had not done it in secret. You may have preferred if it had been a secret thing. Fortunately the Lord is not afraid of your enemies, whether they be strangers or people of your household. Your destiny in God is a prepared blessing but the enemy is watching to see how you would sit down and partake of it.

There was no coherent theology of the devil and his periodic attacks in the Old Testament. So each individual with a significant destiny was steeped in battles or saw his neighbour as his enemy. Whereas the devil has always been the real enemy of mankind, he was in hiding in the Old Testament. Jesus Christ came and removed the veil in the New Testament and exposed him for who he really is. He is a thief, a liar, a killer and a destroyer (John 10:10 ; 8:44). If he can't lie to you successfully, he will try to steal your destiny. And if he can't steal it, he will try to kill it. But even more, if he fails at killing you or what you stand for in the program of God he will try to destroy you completely.

The real battles of your life are not against flesh and blood; (2 Cor.10:3-5) men and women you face everyday or interact with. Your battles are against demonic entities who have got a sniff of where you are heading.

The moment it is uttered from the mouth of God it is no longer a secret anymore. Knowing fully well that it is going to bring blessings to your life, and others, the devil will not fold his hands and watch you become a blessing without trying to resist you.

He will create negative circumstances to demoralise you and make you doubt the integrity of what God has spoken to you. Do you think he is going to use strangers to attack and discourage you? No. Your close relations and acquaintances are the ones he will use through jealousy and envy.

Hear David's experience in this regard:

Psalm 55:12-14 (NKJV)
For it is not an enemy who reproaches me; Then I could bear it. Nor is it one who hates me who has exalted himself against me; Then I could hide from him. [13] But it was you, a man my equal, My companion and my acquaintance. [14] We took sweet counsel together, And walked to the house of God in the throng.

And I've got news for you: God will not hold you back from facing those battles. He will not completely keep the devil at bay for you. He will use him to develop your fighting mentality, though He will not allow him to go beyond the borders of your endurance. God knows your limit. Don't you say, 'I can't take it anymore'. If it is still coming it's because you can overcome it as long as your focus is right on the Captain of your salvation.

Remember, you have actually won the war so the battles are simply the steps taking you to your winning destination, therefore enjoy the aroma of the victory Christ has given you.

Again, the key to victory for you in every battle is the patience of God. Hold your ground, standing on what God has promised you. Keep declaring it openly in the face of adversities and it won't be long when the hold of Satan will be broken and you break through into your prepared blessing. The book of Hebrew speaks particularly to this patience required of you while you are waiting to come into what God has promised you:

Hebrews 10:35-39 (NKJV)
Therefore do not cast away your confidence, which has great reward. [36] For you have need of endurance, so that after you have done the will

of God, you may receive the promise:
[37] "For yet a little while, And He who is coming
will come and will not tarry. [38] Now the just
shall live by faith; But if anyone draws back,
My soul has no pleasure in him."[39] But we are
not of those who draw back to perdition, but of
those who believe to the saving of the soul.

King James Version (KJV) says of verse 36: '*For*
you have need of patience...' I think they are
both saying the same thing. Another word you
can also use for that is '*perserverance*' which,
I may also say, in today's language is 'mental
toughness.'

All these words depict the expected mental state
of a soldier involved in a war.

Reality of spiritual warfare

I recently noticed here in the Western world,
Media propaganda that systematically feeds the
civilian populace of tragedies of war in Iraq and
Afghanistan all in the name of democracy. The
problem I have with this kind of news is that the
majority of the people being fed with this bar-
rage of war news are not mentally prepared to

receive or digest it.

Paul in his letter to Timothy warns him not to get caught in this obvious trap:

2 Timothy 2:3-4 (NKJV)
You therefore must endure hardship as a good soldier of Jesus Christ. [4] No one engaged in warfare entangles himself with the affairs of this life, that he may please him who enlisted him as a soldier.

What this means for you as a believer is that whether you will admit it or not you have been conscripted into the army of God as a soldier and the nature of your warfare is spiritual. It is not physical. Now that you realise you are a soldier contesting for the purposes of God for your life, you may as well wake up and take your place and weapons and fight to live for the honour of God for your life. A lot of believers are not aware of the spiritual reality of their warfare. They are entangled in the affairs of this life to their detriment.

They are holding on to their spiritual weapon with one hand, and at the same time, clinging to what this world can offer them by being earthly focused but heavenly forgetful.

The way Paul says it is the way it really is. You cannot allow distractions whilst you are in a war. You have got to be resolute and focused. Broken focus is a prerequisite to spiritual and mental break down. You have to keep your eyes on Jesus resolutely, not allowing for distractions in the same way Jesus Christ Himself set His eyes, like a flint, on the joy of what was promised and set before Him:

Hebrews 12:2 (NKJV)
looking unto Jesus, the author and finisher of our faith, who for the joy that was set before Him endured the cross, despising the shame, and has sat down at the right hand of the throne of God.

There you see the word again: endurance. If Jesus endured you have got to learn to endure. But the secret to Jesus' endurance was his focus. If He were not focused on what His Father had promised Him, He would not have been able to endure and despise the shame and ridicule of the enemy against His life. The same applies to everyone who completed their race or fulfilled their destiny in the Bible. The principle applies to you too.

Weapons of your warfare

Honestly this chapter would not be complete without talking about the weapons of your warfare if you have come to terms with the reality of the warfare you have been enlisted. However, I do not want to repeat the obvious which you are quite familiar with if you have been a believer for some time now:

Ephesians 6:11-18 (NKJV)
Put on the whole armor of God, that you may be able to stand against the wiles of the devil. [12] For we do not wrestle against flesh and blood, but against principalities, against powers, against the rulers of the darkness of this age, against spiritual hosts of wickedness in the heavenly places. [13] Therefore take up the whole armor of God, that you may be able to withstand in the evil day, and having done all, to stand.

[14] Stand therefore, having girded your waist with truth, having put on the breastplate of righteousness, [15] and having shod your feet with the preparation of the gospel of peace; [16] above all, taking the shield of faith with which you will be able to quench all the fiery darts of the wicked one. [17] And take the helmet of salvation, and

the sword of the Spirit, which is the word of God;
[18] praying always with all prayer and suppli-
cation in the Spirit, being watchful to this end
with all perseverance and supplication for all the
saints.

A lot of us can quote the passage verbatim but I
have been a believer long enough to realise that
many forget these weapons when the push comes
to shove; when the enemy comes with a spate of
attacks. It's like a soldier frantically looking for
the trigger on his rifle when he spots the enemy.
Yes, he knows he has a rifle but he just can't
remember where the trigger is located on the rifle at the sight of the enemy. This analogy may
sound far-fetched but it has a ring of truth to it.

What on earth could make a soldier forget such
an important thing when it matters the most?
He has not been practising using his rifle! One
thing that will make you ready, steady and fir-
ing all the time can be glimpsed from the life of
David. Remember, there was not a long list of
weapons detailed, as in the passage above, that
David used when faced with Goliath or the bear
or the lion. But one thing that made whatever
he had in his hand turn into a weapon capable
of yielding maximum damage to the enemy was

that he knew the presence of God.

Listen to this: David knew God's presence like no one else did in our day today even though he did not live in the New Testament. The implication is that it's possible for you to walk with God today to the extent that you will not break a sweat when the heat of the battles is at its hottest.

Psalm 27 perfectly illustrates the truth of this matter:

Psalm 27:1-14 (NKJV)
A Psalm of David.
The Lord is my light and my salvation; Whom shall I fear? The Lord is the strength of my life; Of whom shall I be afraid? [2] When the wicked came against me to eat up my flesh, My enemies and foes, they stumbled and fell. [3] Though an army may encamp against me, my heart shall not fear; Though war should rise against me,
in this I will be confident. [4] One thing I have desired of the Lord, That will I seek: That I may dwell in the house of the Lord all the days of my life, To behold the beauty of the Lord, and to inquire in His temple. [5] For in the time of trouble He shall hide me in His pavilion; In the

secret place of His tabernacle He shall hide me; He shall set me high upon a rock. [6] And now my head shall be lifted up above my enemies all around me; Therefore I will offer sacrifices of joy in His tabernacle; I will sing, yes, I will sing praises to the Lord. [7] Hear, O Lord, when I cry with my voice!Have mercy also upon me, and answer me. [8] When You said, "Seek My face," My heart said to You, "Your face, Lord, I will seek." [9] Do not hide Your face from me; Do not turn Your servant away in anger; You have been my help; Do not leave me nor forsake me, O God of my salvation.

[10] When my father and my mother forsake me, Then the Lord will take care of me. [11] Teach me Your way, O Lord, And lead me in a smooth path, because of my enemies. [12] Do not deliver me to the will of my adversaries; For false witnesses have risen against me, And such as breathe out violence.[13] I would have lost heart, unless I had believed that I would see the goodness of the Lord In the land of the living. [14] Wait on the Lord; Be of good courage, And He shall strengthen your heart; Wait, I say, on the Lord!

Did you notice the picture verses two and three are trying to paint? David was surrounded by enemies on every side, ready to devour him like a piece of meat. Did you also notice his response in verse four? He was not looking for his whole armour: waist belt of truth, breastplate of righteousness, feet shod with the preparation of the gospel of peace, the shield of faith, helmet of salvation and the sword of the spirit. No. There was only one thing he desired when faced with battle, declared by a myriad of enemies. He desired the presence of God and to dwell in His presence, not just some days of his life but all the days of his life.

That is the secret of putting on the whole armour of God: being in God's presence everyday. Not forgetting His presence when everything is rosy only to scurry back in when the tide changes. J P Timmons in his book, *'Mysterious secrets of the dark kingdom'* asserted a statement that I think will bless you as it has blessed me: *"there are no spiritual batteries."* In other words, yesterday's time you had in God's presence is not enough for today. Cultivate the habit of being in His presence everyday and you won't need to bother about whether you have put on your weapons for warfare or how you might use them.

Finally, notice the result for David of dwelling in God's presence and enquiring in His temple daily:

[5] For in the time of trouble He shall hide me in His pavilion; In the secret place of His tabernacle He shall hide me; He shall set me high upon a rock. [6] And now my head shall be lifted up above my enemies all around me; Therefore I will offer sacrifices of joy in His tabernacle; I will sing, yes, I will sing praises to the Lord...
Psalm 27:5-6(NKJV)

There can be no worse time of trouble like the time the enemy faces you with his arsenal intending to bring you down and cut you short of your blessing in God. Yet that is the time to put on the principal of your weapon, delighting in the presence of God. Whatever makes you run helter skelter in times of battle and disqualifies you from being recognised as a man of war has already denied you of His presence up until that moment.

CHAPTER FIVE

Prudent in speech

"...prudent in speech..."
1 Samuel 16:18 (NKJV)

I have often wondered why the quality of prudence of speech mattered in the observation of
David by the servant who introduced him to
King Saul. The question is: how well was David
known by this servant to have served as his PR
at this juncture in David's life? He definitely
had some information about David to leave an
impression with King Saul. He must also have
been God's plant to engineer David's introduction to the palace. Did it really matter that David was prudent in speech?

What significance was the use of David's manner of speech in the palace court? I estimate that
it's all about courtesy and nothing more. But it
would have to be more than just courtesy if you
realised that David was going to be privileged
to inside information from within Saul's palace.
He was going to see the King up close beyond
the façade of public protocols. He was going to
be in a position where he could see the good,
the bad and the ugly sides of the king within his
harem. And he had better not be a tale and tell
person who might spill beans to the public.

Thesaurus: English (U.K), the Microsoft Word Dictionary Software, uses a string of words to describe the quality of prudence. Among many words used I like the following: *carefulness, discretion, caution, forethought and good sense*. All these are desirable qualities to have for the one who is going to be in the presence of the King. Princess Diana, former Princess of Wales, was involved in a ghastly motor accident that took her life. For a considerable length of time after her death, the British tabloid newspapers sensationalised every piece of information that filtered through from her staff about her private dealings. There was, in particular, the case of her former butler who publicly aired a lot of her dirty linen. I guess that was not being prudent in speech; all for the sake of money.

Character is the issue here

What this borders on is the issue of trustworthiness, integrity, loyalty and the like. Can you be trusted with secrets? What secrets? To become great you have to dine with the greats. And the greats are not always great in private. There are moments when they let their guard down; when you see them in their humanity.

When you are privileged to witness such moments can you keep secrets? Can you protect the king's back when his armour is down? You see, when God gives you opportunities to have access to the greats because of His program to prepare you for the palace, can you please keep your mouth closed when you are disappointed with some things you see of them in their privacy?

My wife and I were privileged to serve a man of God for many years prior to God releasing us to start our own ministry. Sometimes we have had to sit back and do a mental S.W.O.T. analysis of our experience in that ministry to know what 'Strengths' we gathered in our years of service. What 'Weaknesses' we were exposed to that needed to be jettisoned lest they be repeated in our own lives. What great 'Opportunities' God entrusted us with through the man of God and what 'Threats' we needed to be aware of?

Now, this is not an exercise for a committee of people - it is strictly a review of our learning experiences. It is amazing to discover how influential leaders are over those who serve them. We even went further to look into our individual backgrounds to see what excess baggage we brought from our family upbringings. All is not doom and gloom though.

It was Apostle James who said that your mouth or tongue is the harness of your whole life: We all stumble in many ways. *If anyone is never at fault in what he says, he is a perfect man, able to keep his whole body in check...*[James 3:2 (ANIV)].

Invariably, what this is saying is that, if you are prudent in speech you will be prudent with your whole life. If you are discreet with your words it is an indication you will be discreet with your life. Who you really are is the issue here. Your speech gives you away. Your language tells what is in your heart because whatever is in your heart is already in your life. I have known a few people, in my years of pastoring people of God, who had verbal diarrhea; always running and never stopping. You just needed to ask them: 'How are you?' You would get an ear full of the necessary and the unnecessary. They just didn't know where and when to stop. For such a person, next time I saw them, I would always be cautious of asking, 'How are you?' for concern of being tied down with stories of woe upon woe.

Sword in your mouth

Recently I discovered that each time Jesus Christ is depicted with the sword in the book of Revelation, He is not actually holding the sword in His Hand. The sword is in His mouth:

Revelation 1:16 (KJV)
And he had in his right hand seven stars: and out of his mouth went a sharp twoedged sword: and his countenance was as the sun shineth in his strength.

Revelation 2:16 (NKJV)
Repent, or else I will come to you quickly and will fight against them with the sword of My mouth.

Revelation 19:15 (NKJV)
Now out of His mouth goes a sharp sword, that with it He should strike the nations. And He Himself will rule them with a rod of iron. He Himself treads the winepress of the fierceness and wrath of Almighty God.

Revelation 19:21 (NKJV)
And the rest were killed with the sword which proceeded from the mouth of Him who sat on the horse. And all the birds were filled with their

flesh.

The significance of this discovery for me is the fact that it emphasises, a great deal, the awesome power of the tongue. Yes, I have read it in the book of Proverbs that *life and death lie in the power of the tongue* (Proverbs 18:21) and other related verses which show the great power of the tongue. But this discovery in the book of Revelation, for me, vividly illustrates the truth of the power. So what lesson can you derive from this truth? It is simple. You can kill with your mouth without any physical evidence to convict you of murder.

Now there are other implications for this discovery which I do not intend to address at this juncture like the effects of God's Word in your mouth against the powers of darkness, the importance of confessing God's Word over your situations and circumstances etc. These topics shall be dealt with later, either in this book or in another book.

However, if you don't know how to give life through your speech on the way to the palace, you will definitely not know how to preserve life with your mouth when you have ascended the throne. This means you have got to work on yourself. The palace is not meant for showing how powerful you are to the detriment of your subjects; it is meant to be the seat of service, in your sphere of influence, to the people God will bring your way.

Managing Your Anger

Oftentimes when a person has problems controlling his or her mouth, he also has an underlining problem with unresolved issues which manifest into anger. The way some people deal with unresolved issue is either to repress their anger or blow up with it. It simply depends on how you have internalised the matters of concern. Eventually, when the issue comes to surface you may not be able to control the tidal wave of emotions and the verbal outbursts that result.

I was brought up in a culture that does not encourage younger ones to express their displeasure at injustice from their elders. In fact, it could get so bad that the younger ones were made to apologise to their elders even when it was glaringly obvious that the elders were at fault. The rationale for this was that the older ones were always right and if they were wrong at all, the younger ones should just accept it as a way of life and they should not make any noise by trying to voice their opinion. But you see, this fosters anger in the hearts of many young people who have been wronged by their older counterparts and it is a panacea for future trouble. Why? If issues are not resolved but kept under the carpet they have a way of oozing out in another form. You know, the Scriptures say that *'whatsoever is hidden shall be made revealed'*. (Matthew 10:26)

Some of these issues become revealed in sicknesses and diseases because the mind has not got the capacity to harbour ill will for long. As a result, it manifests as a disease or illness, in the body of the one carrying ill will. This is what is known as psychosomatic diseases. However, when the issues are dealt with the diseases also disappear provided they have not done much damage to the body. This is also the reason God asks us to forgive whoever offends us. Just think about it. Whatever God asks us to do is not first of all for His benefit but ours. Bitterness, anger, unresolved issues and all other negative emotions don't harm God – they harm us. Whenever you hold on to negative emotions, you become the victim. Someone once defined bitterness 'as a poison you drink and expecting your enemy to drop dead.' How possible is that? It is a fallacy.

In my late teenage years I was once a very angry person and that was because I could not express my disappointment and anger at some of the injustices I saw around me. Now, understand that people are imperfect and that you will always have people's imperfections thrust in your face. You could have much difficulty dealing with them if you are an idealist and immature.

As a twenty year old who had lived with different families and been exposed to different situations I was frustrated and angry that the whole world did not dance to my tune. But that was a day dream really. Not knowing how to deal with my disappointments almost caused me one of the relationships that had blessed me so much up until the incident occurred. I expressed my mind without being concerned about what effects my tirade could have on my perceived enemy. But thank God for the maturity expressed by my 'Uncle' which also aided in my becoming wiser.

The incident eventually led to me philosophis-ing that there are better ways to express my opinions no matter how grieved I may be about the situation.

The Scriptures say, *'Be not hasty in thy spirit to be angry: for anger resteth in the bosom of fools.'* Eccles. 7:9 (KJV). The one who allows anger to fester in his heart has the potential to do damage with his virulent words. So the quicker issues are dealt with in wisdom the better, and wisdom will also prevent the possibility of becoming poi-sonous with words as a result of anger.

David had not yet been thrust into the full glare of publicity when the servant of Saul testified of him as being prudent in speech. There must have been some stories circulating around Bethlehem to attest to this quality. Maybe it had gotten through to some servants' ears in the palace, how he handled the apparent rejection meted out to him by his whole household, when Prophet Samuel came calling on the family to anoint a replacement king for Saul under the pretense of offering sacrifices to God (1 Samuel 16:1-13).

But then if that was the case there was no way he would have been recommended by the servant of Saul as a therapy harp player for a possessed king. Perhaps, the only possible reason for this testimony was the way David handled the news of his heroic exploits of slaying the bear and the lion. He probably down played the news fallout of these victories, not wanting to arrogate anything of significance to himself. Otherwise, he would not have gone back to look after the sheep despite being recognised as a bear and a lion slayer.

Esteem yourself in the right proportion

The point in this is that David esteemed himself lightly in the sight of men even as a teenager with an amazing track record of victories under his belt. If this had not been the case he could have advertised his prowess and overplayed his own importance. Those who seek to promote themselves shall not be innocent when tested with prudence of speech. A desire to be famous will make anyone to fall into a trap of pride and over-inflation of one's self importance.

This will ultimately make the person esteem himself more highly than he ought to. Have you ever wondered why Jesus Christ in the New Testament would perform a miracle obvious to everybody and still commanded His disciples not to tell anybody? Take for instance the case of Jairus' daughter raised from the dead (Mark 5:21-43). If you painted a mental picture of the narrative you would see that everybody already knew where Jesus was heading after the ruler of the synagogue came pleading for Him to come and lay His hand on his daughter so that she might live. And while on the way He was interrupted by the woman with the issue of blood. By this time news came to Jairus, who was leading Jesus to his house, not to bother the Master anymore because his daughter had died. Before Jairus could reply Jesus put in a word of encouragement to him, 'Be not afraid, only believe' (Mark 5:36). Let us read the rest of the story as Jesus reached Jairus' house:

Luke 8:51-56 (KJV)
And when he came into the house, he suffered no man to go in, save Peter, and James, and John, and the father and the mother of the maiden. [52] And all wept, and bewailed her: but he said, Weep not; she is not dead, but sleepeth. [53] And they laughed him to scorn, knowing that she was dead. [54] And he put them all out, and

took her by the hand, and called, saying, Maid, arise. [55] And her spirit came again, and she arose straightway: and he commanded to give her meat. [56] And her parents were astonished: but he charged them that they should tell no man what was done.

Did you read that last verse? Now, how on earth would Jesus say *'that they should tell no man what was done'*? The truth of the matter is that everybody already knew what was done. This statement only revealed the attitude of Jesus towards fame. He was not looking for fame but fame was always looking for Him. If He were looking for fame, He would have blown the miracle out of proportion and commandeered his disciples to engage the services of the local media groups and have them publish it in all nooks and corners of the land. He would probably also have demanded that the beneficiary family take out an advertisement slot in the local newspapers to testify to what the Lord had done for them. All these things sound legitimate but the motives may not be right.

Now, I am not saying anything is wrong in advertising miracles for crusades and what have you. What I am saying is that something is wrong if you are besotted with self promotion in order to be famous under the guise of promoting the gospel. Such a person shall not rightly esteem himself but will get taken over by a competitive spirit and will not be prudent with his speech.

There was no occasion again, apart from intimating Saul, in the whole of the Bible when David referred to his killing of the lion or the bear, not even in the Psalms which chronicled his various trials and tribulations and his responses to them emotionally. But he recognised this same quality of prudence of speech in Benaiah, the son of Jehoiada when he submitted his CV for a position among the mighty men of David and David subsequently set him over his guard as the Chief Security Officer (CSO):

1 Chronicles 11:22-25 (KJV)
Benaiah the son of Jehoiada, the son of a valiant man of Kabzeel, who had done many acts; he slew two lionlike men of Moab: also he went down and slew a lion in a pit in a snowy day. [23] And he slew an Egyptian, a man of great stature, five cubits high; and in the Egyptian's hand was a spear like a weaver's beam; and he went down to him with a staff, and plucked the spear out of the Egyptian's hand, and slew him with his

own spear. [24] These things did Benaiah the son of Jehoiada, and had the name among the three mighties. [25] Behold, he was honourable among the thirty, but attained not to the first three: and David set him over his guard.

CHAPTER SIX

A handsome person

"...and a handsome person..."
1 Samuel 16:18 (NKJV)

Physical appearances matter too

You would have thought that physical appearance does not matter in the equation of success in life. But I conclude that God thinks otherwise. If not, He would not have allowed this to be a factor to be included in the considered profile of David at the point of his entrance to the palace. Make no mistake about it: first impressions matter. You never ever really get a second chance to create a first impression. Previously in our text there appears a statement that sounds contrary to what we are considering now:

But the Lord said to Samuel, "Do not look at his appearance or at the height of his stature, because I have refused him. For the Lord does not see as man sees; for man looks at the outward appearance, but the Lord looks at the heart."
1 Samuel 16:7 (NKJV)

Well, it is really not contradictory if you consider that God looks beyond the physical appearance to the real issue of the heart because He is a Spirit. Even though man is also a spirit in essence but the first contact between man and man is always a physical one. Moreover, you could never be invited to a state dinner and show up looking your worst. You would go to town and dress yourself up even if you had to go and hire a tuxedo. It's all about first appearances and perceptions.

Prophet Samuel's first impression of David was that he was *'ruddy, with bright eyes and good-looking'* (1 Samuel 16:12). This most probably means he had a special physical feature different from the rest of the pack. But that is not all. To have a special outstanding feature is one thing, to keep it glowing is another. If you had seen people working as sheep farmers may be you would have an idea of their tendency to smell and look like the sheep they reared.

It would definitely require a great deal of effort to keep up a good physical appearance if you were a shepherd boy. Regardless of whatever profession you might be engaged in, beauty cannot be hidden even if splattered with murk and mire. David must have indeed been a beauty to behold. Absalom, his third son (1 Chron.3:2), was also distinctly attractive. David had a soft spot for Absalom in his heart.

Absalom became indulgent beyond acceptable
reasons unlike any other child of David. Maybe
he was a carbon copy of his father. Absalom was
a handsome man. A chip off the old block! The
Living Bible puts it succinctly:

Now no one in Israel was such a handsome speci-
men of manhood as Absalom, and no one else
received such praise.
2 Samuel 14:25 (Living Bible)

Defining beauty

'Beauty,' it is often said, 'is in the eye of the
beholder.' Beauty is so esoteric that it defies
definition yet when you see it you know it. What
constitutes beauty? What shape of the face do
you have to have to be accepted as beautiful?
What is recognised as beautiful in one part
of the world may not be what is considered
beautiful in another part of the world. I have
oftentimes been disappointed by the result of
the beauty pageant shows paraded on terrestrial
television or in the newspaper. Most winners
in my estimation do not count for the most
beautiful woman or lady available. Yet, to the
judges of the pageant shows their choice of

winner most probably met their criteria. But, what criteria? That is the question no one is able to answer.The world is presently obsessed with looking after the outer shell of man, his body. A wise man once observed, 'The best of man is just glorified dust after all.' Why bother looking after the dust then? It is the earth suit for the spirit of man. The Bible metaphorically calls it the temple of God for each believer (1 Cor.3:16; 6:19) and encourages each believer to keep it holy and undefiled without sin of fornication or adultery.

On the other hand since the metaphoric language of the temple was used for the human body, it presupposed that it must be adorned and made glorious like the temple of Solomon was glorious in appearance, and of whose glory no other physical temple had ever been compared. Now, if you think you are beautiful then you are beautiful. Or if you think you are handsome then you are handsome. I do not agree that God makes junk. All things created by Him were declared good. In actual fact, the pronouncement at the end of the sixth day of creation from the Genesis account was that it was 'very good' whereas every other day of creation leading to the sixth day had only been declared 'good':

Genesis 1:31 (NKJV)
Then God saw everything that He had made, and indeed it was very good. So the evening and the morning were the sixth day.

It is no accident that God reserved His best adjective to describe His creation until you were formed. You are the crown of God's creation. And your creation invoked the best adjective possible for God to describe His admiration of you. On the other hand I am aware that the preoccupation of the devil is to destroy all that God has made beautiful (John 10:10). But whose report will you believe? I would rather believe the report of the Lord. You are beautiful for all the situations of your life (Psalm 48:2 KJV).

Deception of physical beauty

There is a deception that results from being obsessed with physical beauty. This is what the 'vanity' of the beauty business industry capitalises on. Whatever makes anyone become addicted to improve his outer look through cosmetic surgery without spending a dime to look after his inner man is a warped value focus. Yet this is what today's Hollywood thrives on. It's all about looking good and looking good physically. Yet nobody really bothers to care for what their inner man looks like. They wouldn't even know it if they saw it.

The Scriptures say though our outward man, that is the physical man, perishes, our inward man is renewed daily (2 Cor.4:16). The question then is: why invest heavily in something where value deteriorates, with the passage of time, when you could reap an eternal reward by building the inner man? The Scripture is not saying to neglect your outward appearance but rather that things should be done in moderation. Balance is the name of the game here. If a believer is willing to spend thousands of pounds to improve his physique how much is he willing to spend to feed his spirit comparatively? If the scale tilts to the favour of looking good physically, then deception has set in.

The conclusion of such a misplaced priority is beautifully stated by the following verse:

WHOSE END IS DESTRUCTION, whose god is their belly, and whose glory is in their shame-

-WHO SET THEIR MIND ON EARTHLY THINGS. [20] For our citizenship is in heaven, from which we also eagerly wait for the Savior, the Lord Jesus Christ, [21] WHO WILL TRANS-FORM OUR LOWLY BODY THAT IT MAY BE CONFORMED TO HIS GLORIOUS BODY, according to the working by which He is able even to subdue all things to Himself...
Philippians 3:19-21 (NKJV)

Putting everything in perspective, the theology of the Old Testament did not allow for the understanding of the inner man in the same degree that we have now understood it to be. Thus the servant of Saul who included the physical beauty of David in his profile submission to Saul did not get it wrong completely. He was only walking according to his limited knowledge.

Believers should not allow themselves to be run over by the culture of the day. *'Be not conformed to this world but be transformed by the renewing of your mind so that you may prove that which is the good, acceptable and perfect will of God,'* (Rom. 12:2) is the injunction given to today's believers in the face of ever-present allures of misplaced values.

Basic hygienic skills will suffice

Without extravagance basic hygienic rules of cleanliness in appearance both in private and public life should do the trick. These are skills that good home training and upbringing would have instilled in each one of us. It is good to brush one's teeth regularly and visit the dentist at least once a year to maintain good oral health. If you dress well and carry yourself well at first appearance when your opportunity shows up only to leave a lasting, foul tasting impression of bad breath; all because basic hygiene is not observed, of what use will the opportunity amount to?

The use of good deodorant is not a sign of worldliness. A good fragrance enhances a good aura. It is not a sign of backsliding to use a scented roller for sweaty armpits. It is all about enhancing your image. It all adds to your handsome or beauty factor.

CHAPTER SEVEN

And the Lord is with him

"...; and the Lord is with him..."
1 Samuel 16:18 (NKJV)

This is the most important factor in all we have considered so far. This is the God factor. This is the one that crowns everything else. You see, everything else we have been discussing up to now will avail to nothing if this factor is not included in the equation of opportunity in your life.

Your part; and God's part

In everything you experience in life you will always have your part to play and God will always have His part to play. The idea that everything is in the hands of God will not work. That is a cop out from accepting personal responsibility. In fact it goes against every good theology you will ever learn from the Bible. God has always sought for the obedience and cooperation of His people:

'If you are *willing* and *obedient,* You shall eat the good of the land;'
Isaiah 1:19 (NKJV),

'If they *obey* and *serve* Him, They shall spend their days in prosperity, And their years in pleasures. [12] But if they do not obey, They shall perish by the sword, And they shall die without knowledge.'
Job 36:11-12 (NKJV)

'But this is what I commanded them, saying, '*Obey* My voice, and I will be your God, and you shall be My people. And walk in all the ways that I have commanded you, that it may be well with you.'
Jeremiah 7:23 (NKJV)

'*Draw* near to God and He will draw near to you. Cleanse your hands, you sinners; and purify your hearts, you double-minded.'
James 4:8 (NKJV)

All of the above, and many similar Scripture quotations point to one thing. God's promises of blessing are conditional and dependent upon obedience. Hitherto, you may not have heard the whole truth: God desires utter obedience to His commandments. To fall short in wilful obedience is to court His displeasure and forfeit His best. God requires active obedience as opposed to passive obedience that borders on fatalism saying 'God will do what He will do'.

Yes, He will do what He will do but He may not do it with whom He originally intended to do it with, if the person is in wilful disobedience.

God never shirks His responsibility. At a point in David's life when God established a covenant with him, He called His unchangeableness the 'sure mercies of David' (Psalm 89; Is.55:3). However, He put in a caveat that if any of David's descendants disobeyed Him He would punish the culprit and later draw the repentant to Himself afterwards.

The presence of the Lord

When a child of God is in fellowship with God, he will be aware of His presence. But if he is no longer experiencing His presence your guess is as good as mine as to who moved away. God has promised never to leave His own. Jesus reiterated this assertion in the New Testament: *'For He Himself has said, "I will never leave you nor forsake you."* 'Hebrews 13:5 (NKJV) (Referencing Deut.31:6, 8; Joshua 1:5). David Bryant in his *Kingdom Dynamics* contribution to The New Spirit Filled Life Bible passage of Ephesians 3:14-

21 distinguishes three kinds of God's presence, based on the Puritans usage of the phrase during the Great Awakenings: First was 'essential presence' (that is God is always with us). Second was His 'cultivated presence' (which comes as the believer grows to know and walk with God daily) and lastly, the most desired of them all, the 'manifest presence' of God. He elaborated further that prayer for revival is a call to this manifest presence, something wonderfully beyond the first two.

After having observed this, the next question is which presence is necessary to take you to the next level of promotion and fits the description of David? I am of the opinion that the second one was what the servant of Saul was referring to when he was introducing David to King Saul in absentia.

This is what is needed for you also to experience God daily. It comes as a result of seeking Him daily, it does not come by sporadic and inconsistent fellowship with God. In actual fact this is what will launch you to the level of manifest presence eventually. The deepening of your relationship with God is through fellowship.

This also was what Abraham, the progenitor of David, did that caused God to bless and increase him. For a better exposé of this study in the life of Abraham please read my book, 'Abraham In The Mirror.'

Favour is a function of God's 'cultivated presence'

Favour by its nature is a form of manifest presence. When you are head hunted for a higher position you did not apply for and, unknowingly to others, you are being edged to the fulfilment of your destiny - that is favour. Favour is all you need to get there. When your name is made mention of for rewards forgotten and abandoned, but now resurrected for your sake, in great circles of repute and substance - that is favour. When others fight for you without your knowledge so you can be blessed and promoted - that is favour.

Do you realise that a day's favour can wipe away a thousand years of hard labour and replace it with laughter and joy? That is what you need to ascend the throne prepared for you to reign. You might feel forgotten and forsaken as others look at you and rub their noses because you are covered with sheep's odour, don't succumb to self pity at all, keep revelling in the cultivated presence of God until your fullness of time comes!

David was known for the richness of his relationship with God. I think David was an Old Testament saint in New Testament glory. The sweet psalmist of Israel was ahead of his time. You can do much more today than David was able to do in his walk with God because the Holy Spirit dwells within you.

God's favourite child

Don't subscribe to the erroneous, though popular, belief that God does not have favourite children. He does! When God favours you, then you have become His favourite child. What has often been mis-interpreted is the fact that God is not a Respecter of persons:

Then Peter opened his mouth and said: "In truth I perceive that God shows no partiality. [35] But in every nation whoever fears Him and works righteousness is accepted by Him."
Acts 10:34-35 (NKJV)

The truth of the above statement must be considered within context. Half truths are as deadly as a blatant lie! God gives honour to those who reverence, obey and serve Him. There it is plainly stated in the above passage that *'in every nation whoever fears Him and works righteousness is accepted by Him.'* So the key to becoming God's favourite child is to fear Him and do what is right as much as it lies within you.

Hear is another passage that reveals what your possibilities are in God: But He gives more grace. Therefore He says:

"God resists the proud, But gives grace to the humble."
James 4:6 (NKJV)

More grace means more favour is dished out to the humble. The humble are the doers of His Word. They are not mere listeners or readers of His Word but doers! As a result, they receive more grace meaning their portion is above the rest of the pack. This is how you become God's favourite child. This does not mean you have become perfect; rather, it shows you are growing in Him and in His grace (2 Pet.3:18).

On the other hand it is frightening to think how God in His might and power will resist the proud. For, if God resists anyone because of arrogance and pride only through repentance and mercy can the proud be delivered.

To remain God's favourite child maintain a tender heart and be quick to obey Him (Psalm 51:17). When your opportunity comes you will have been adequately prepared for it. Remember, when opportunity meets preparation - success, a **Royal Invitation To The Palace**, is the result.

Salvation Prayer

Father, Your Word says that "Whosoever shall call upon the name of the Lord shall be saved". I take You at Your Word, acknowledge that I am a sinner and confess that Jesus is my Lord and Saviour. I believe in my heart that You raised Him from the dead. By faith in Your Word, I receive salvation now and have been translated into the Kingdom of Your dear Son. Thank You for coming into my heart and for being Lord over my life.

In Jesus Name I pray

Amen